# RAINBOW

D0459189

FAMILY
MATTERS

# You and the Rules in Your Family

**Lea MacAdam**

the rosen publishing group's
rosen
central

*To Helen and Monty*

Published in 2001 by The Rosen Publishing Group, Inc.
29 East 21st Street, New York, NY 10010

First Edition

**Library of Congress Cataloging-in-Publication Data**

MacAdam, Lea.
   You and the rules in your family / Lea MacAdam. — 1st ed.
      p.  cm. — (Family matters)
   Includes bibliographical references and index.
   ISBN 0-8239-3350-4 (lib bdg.)
 1. Parent and teenager—Juvenile literature. 2. Teenagers—conduct of life—Juvenile literature. [1. Conduct of life. 2. Family life.] I. Title. II. Family matters (New York, N.Y.)
   HQ799.15 .M28 2000
   306.874—dc21

                                                   00-010123

# Contents

If you want to get along with others, you will have to obey certain rules.

# Introduction

"Playing by the rules." "Bending the rules." "Rules are made to be broken."

Have you ever heard these expressions before? They are pretty common in day-to-day conversation. The constant use of these and other similar expressions only goes to show how big a part rules play in our lives. Whether we are making them, breaking them, or following them, there is no escaping rules. Without them, life would be a big mess. Imagine a world with no laws, no regulations, no controls of any kind. It could be pretty scary.

Rules are funny things. Nobody much likes making them and enforcing them. And often people don't particularly like following them. People find some rules to be unfair, unnecessary, or just plain stupid. But if you want to get along with others—at home, at school, and out in the world—you will have to learn to obey certain rules that make these situations more orderly, organized, safer, and civilized.

When you're young, you have a lot of rules to follow. That's just the way it is. You're a kid and your parents are responsible for your becoming a good person. To do this, they'll try to teach you how to live and share with others, how to do not just what makes you happy but what makes sense. And though you might disagree, in most cases, your parents know a lot more and have much more experience than you do.

A big part of growing up is learning how to deal with limits. Sometimes, you can get fed up with all the rules your parents make. But in the long run, it is smart to learn how to deal with rules. This book will hopefully help you do just that. We'll look at some common situations that kids your age and their parents might face. And then we'll take a look at the kinds of rules that might apply to these situations. Some rules might make more sense than others. Hopefully, if there is a rule that makes you unhappy, you can talk it over with your parents and come up with a compromise that you can all agree on.

How you and your family get along is very important since you will be a part of your family for your whole life. Part of getting along is learning how to live with rules and understanding why they are in place to begin with. Also, understanding the what and why of your rules will give you a better sense of who your parents are. This is important because family matters, and a family with good communication is likely to have a more healthy relationship.

# The What, How, and Why of Chores

Imagine what life would be like in your house if there were no rules and everybody in your family did exactly what they wanted to do all of the time. After all, nobody likes collecting garbage and taking it outside. Not too many people like washing dishes, scrubbing toilets, or walking the dog when it's pouring rain outside either. If you think your dad really enjoys dusting, think again. There are probably a million things that would amuse him more.

If your parents do such things, it is not because they're fun but because if these tasks don't get done, your entire family will end up living in a messy and disorganized home. And though initially you might think this could be fun, eventually you'll want some order or cleanliness. To make your home function well, your mom or dad, or both, probably have a set of rules they obey to help them organize their time

Few people enjoy washing dishes, but it is an essential chore for maintaining a clean and orderly home.

and get essential family chores done.

These kinds of rules are not necessarily written down. Many of them—such as buying food, paying bills, or emptying the garbage—have probably become a habit. Sometimes however, a parent might make a note of important "things to do" on a sticky yellow Post-It or on a calendar. Your parent does this not because he or she wants to make your life more difficult, but because it is important for your entire family that certain things get done and that they get done on time.

## GETTING OLDER EQUALS HAVING MORE RESPONSIBILITIES

When you were a little kid, your parents were in charge of doing most things around the house. This is normal. After all, they were bigger, smarter, and were quite simply better at vacuuming than you were. However, as you get older, you become capable of doing more. As you grow up, you become more independent. You also have more say in what goes on around your home. In return, you begin to have more responsibilities. Having responsibilities is part and parcel of becoming an adult. You don't want to reach the age of twenty-five and have your parents still doing everything for you. Your parents probably wouldn't be so thrilled by the idea either.

Being responsible means taking care of yourself and others—such as younger siblings—and your home. Your parents will probably put certain rules in place that will help you carry out your responsibilities.

## Chores

A chore is a routine task or job you do around the house. Chores are often tiresome and while they may not be anyone's favorite thing in the world, they have to be done.

In most families, your mom or dad or both do most of the chores. But as you and your siblings grow older, your parents will expect you to do chores as well. When you think about it, this is only fair, since you live with your parents and you don't even have to pay any rent. So even if you do have to rake the leaves, dry the dishes, or keep an eye on your little sister, it's still a pretty good deal.

*When Deeana's mom came home from work and dumped the grocery bags on the kitchen floor, Deeana was in the den watching television.*

"Dee?" called Mrs. Labruce. "Can you come help me with the groceries?"

"Hang on!" yelled Deeana. "I'm watching a Friends rerun."

"Dee, I need help now! And how come you haven't set the table?"

"Mom! I can't hear you! I'm watching TV!"

"And you didn't make rice or heat up the stew either!"

"Mom! I'm missing a really good part!"

"Deeana!" Mrs. Labruce came stomping into the den. "You know that Tuesdays and Thursdays I have to work late. We agreed that you'd set the table and have dinner ready when I got home. Didn't we agree on that?"

"Yeah... yeah...Can't we talk about this later?"

Mrs. Labruce grabbed the remote and switched the television off.

"Hey, Mom!"

"Deeana, why didn't you do your chores?"

"I was tired! I was at school all day!"

"Well guess what? I was at work all day and I'm tired, too. But I still had time to buy groceries for both of us. You live here, too. Is it too much to ask that you help out by setting the table, boiling some rice, and heating up some stew?"

"Well, I wanted to watch Friends!"

"Dee, this household is more important than a TV show. If you do your chores first, I don't mind you watching TV.  But we had an agreement."

*"Alright, alright,"* sighed Deeana, getting to her feet. She went into the kitchen and began putting away the groceries.

## GETTING PAID FOR HOUSEWORK

Some kids get an allowance—a small sum of money—from their parents. Often the allowance is given in return for helping out around the house. Do you think that's a fair deal? Some parents think it is. They think that having an allowance teaches kids about responsibility.

*"Dad,"* said Alex, sauntering into the kitchen. *"I think you should raise my allowance."*

*"Oh, really?"* asked Mr. Milenov, looking up from his bowl of Wheaties. *"And what will you do in return?"*

*"You mean I have to do more stuff around the house? Billy Donahue gets more money than I do and he doesn't have to do anything. His family has a maid."*

*"Well that's nice for Billy and his family. Unfortunately, your mom and I don't make enough money to be able to afford a maid. And if I'm going to up your allowance, maybe you could help out a little more around the house. Is that so unreasonable?"*

*"I guess not,"* muttered Alex. *"What do I have to do?"*

*"Well,"* said Mr. Milenov. *"If you promise to weed and water the garden, mow the lawn, and take the old newspapers and bottles to the recycling box when*

Some kids get an allowance from their parents for doing household tasks.

*the pile gets too big, I'll give you an extra $5 a week. Deal?"*

*"Yeah, I guess."*

*"Do we need this in writing or will a simple handshake do it?"*

*"A simple hand-shake," said Alex. "Oh, and can I have my raise right now?"*

Doing household chores might not be your favorite thing, but it does give you some useful life experience that will help you become an independent adult. For example, Deeana already knows how to cook certain kinds of food. Alex knows a little bit about gardening. Billy Donahue, with his live-in maid, doesn't know how to do any of these things. And later on in his life, when he lives on his own, he may wish that he did know how to do a few things around the house. And though it may be hard to believe, there are actually some people who find it relaxing to do some dusting or to water the plants.

If you and your parents agree to certain rules, it is pretty lousy if you don't fulfill your obligations. How would you feel if your mom promised to drive you to and from soccer practice and then just decided that she had too much other stuff to do or that she was too tired to pick you up? You'd probably feel let down and angry. If it happened more than once, you'd feel that your mom wasn't responsible and that you couldn't count on her.

Mr. Milenov had to get up early and go to work. But he always left Alex's allowance in an envelope on the kitchen table. One day, Alex opened the envelope and found that half of his allowance was missing. Mrs. Milenov was eating granola and doing homework for her night course at college.

"Hey! Dad gypped me!" yelled Alex.

"What's the problem ,Alex?"

"Dad didn't pay me my whole allowance."

"Well, did you do all the chores you were supposed to do?" asked Mrs. Milenov.

"Well..." Alex hesitated. "I cleared the table and folded the laundry. I just didn't get around to mowing the lawn yet."

"And have you seen that overflowing pile of newspapers in the basement? And those weeds in the backyard?"

"I've been busy, Mom!"

"That's too bad, Alex. We're all busy and we get

*things done. I'm sure when you have time to get your chores done, your dad will give you the rest of your allowance."*

## OTHER HOUSEHOLD MEMBERS, OTHER HOUSEHOLD CHORES

Housework is not the only kind of chore for which you might be responsible. And your mom or dad might not be the only ones who require you to pitch in at home. Your household might include other members, such as siblings or pets, who count on you, too.

If you have younger siblings, your parents may ask you to look after them.

### Brothers and Sisters

If you're an older brother or sister, your parents might want you to take on some responsibilities by helping out with your younger siblings. Maybe your mom will ask you to pick up your little brother after school and bring him home safely. Maybe your dad will put you in charge of taking your little sister to her swimming lessons. If you're in charge, this means that you will be responsible for making sure your younger sibling stays safe by following rules that you already know. If you're crossing a street, it's up to you to remind your little brother to look both ways. If you're at home, in the kitchen, it's up to you to tell your little sister not to play with the knobs on the stove and not to put her hand in an open flame, no matter how pretty the flames look. Believe it or not, being responsible and following rules can make you feel good. Knowing that your family members can rely on you will give you a sense of maturity. After all, it's good to be trustworthy.

If you're a younger brother or sister, your parents might want your older siblings to help take care of you. Although your parents make up the rules in your house, when they aren't around it is up to your older brother or sister to make sure that the normal household rules are being followed. Though it may be tempting, don't make his or her life miserable by taking advantage of the fact that your parents aren't home. At the same time, your older siblings shouldn't make your life miserable by inventing rules of their own that you all know your parents wouldn't approve of.

## Pets

Many kids your age have pets. Many other kids your age want pets. There is nothing like having a dog, cat, parakeet, gerbil, or even giant iguana of your own to

There are many responsibilities that come with having a family pet.

play with and talk to. Of course, as you've probably heard a million times before, having a pet is a big responsibility. Regardless of whether the animal in question belongs to just you or to the whole family, there are going to be rules relating to that particular pet. And as full or part owner of Fluffy, Tiger, or Floyd, it is up to you to see that the cat, dog, or parrot in question follows these rules.

If your mother says she doesn't want Max the Labrador in the backyard because he'll go to the bathroom on her favorite roses, don't let Max out. If your dad doesn't want Annie the Angora cat on his bed because she sheds her long fur all over the sheets, don't let Annie into your dad's room. You might think that your parents are being unreasonable, are overreacting, or are being mean to Max and Annie. But if people are going to get along in a home, everybody's likes and dislikes have to be respected. After you've told your sister 84 billion times that you don't want her pet gerbil loose in your room since that time he chewed up the first four months of your diary, would you really be so understanding if she "forgot the rules" and let the little muncher in again?

# Playtime

Once you've cleared off the table, swept the floor, watered the garden, read a story to your younger sister and done all your homework, it's pretty much a given that you'll be allowed to play. Free time, down-time, leisure time—whatever you want to call it, it's an important part of life.

Of course, rules and regulations don't stop just because your chores are done. There is a big difference between kicking back safely and smartly and kicking back stupidly. Also, when you're relaxing at home, you have to remember that you're not the only one in your house. Your parents and siblings might have other things they want to do, such as sleep, do homework, listen to an opera on the radio, or talk to a good friend on the phone. You have to respect what they want to do just as they should respect what you want to do. The only problem is that sometimes not everybody can do what they want at the same time in the same house. If there are no household rules established, conflicts may arise.

## The Television

Most kids your age like to watch a little bit of TV from time to time. There is nothing wrong with that. There are some really good shows out there that are intelligent and interesting and entertaining. Unfortunately, there are even more programs that are dumb, boring, and a big waste of time. Some people can get easily addicted to television. It can happen before you're aware of it. Just sit back in a chair and channel surf. It takes less effort than reading a book, going for a bike ride, or playing a game of softball with your friends.

If your parents feel that you are spending too much time in front of the television set, they could have a point. Television is good in small doses. There are plenty of other activities to take advantage of. Since your parents are in charge of your education and upbringing, they certainly have

Your parents may limit how much television you are allowed to watch.

the right to set limits on how many hours you spend in front of the television. Not only should they have a say in how much you watch, but what you watch as well. There is a lot of violence, sex, and sheer stupidity on television. Not all of it is meant to be watched by someone your age. Just as there are age limits placed on drinking in a bar or getting into an R-rated movie, your parents might want to place limits on the kinds of TV shows you watch.

*Libby's parents thought her television watching was getting out of hand. In the last six months, she had put on ten pounds just from sitting in front of the tube and eating chips and ice cream. She was also not getting much homework done. Her last report card had been pathetic.*

*"Libby, your TV watching is becoming a problem," her mother said to her. "Your father and I have talked it over and we want you to make up a list of eight shows you'd like to watch every week. We want to see the times they are on and we're going to check them out in* TV Guide *to make sure we approve of them. And each day before you turn on the set, you'll have to show either me or your father your homework. If it's not done, no TV."*

*Libby wasn't very happy with this agreement. It was going to be really hard to narrow down all that great stuff on television to just eight programs. Then again, she didn't want to flunk out of seventh grade.*

## The Telephone

Just as addictive as flicking on the television is talking on the phone. A kid who eats, breathes, and lives on the phone is one of the biggest nightmares a parent can have. Whether it's tying up the line for hours, racking up big phone bills, or getting infinite phone calls from friends late at night or in the middle of meals, kids and phones sometimes go together too well for their own (and everybody else's) good.

Of course you're going to want to chat with friends, set up meetings, and catch up on the day's gossip, but you have to remember that others share your house. This means that they share the phone, too. Unless you have call-waiting, it's really infuriating if your mom is trying to call to say her car broke down and she can't get through because you're telling your friend Mitzi how cute Roger Baker is. It could even be dangerous if it turns out your mom was in an accident. And what if you have other siblings who like to blab as much as you do? Not only will

A kid who spends too much time on the telephone can cause a lot of aggravation for other family members.

your line always be busy, but your house will be full of kids fighting for who gets the phone next and for how long.

If your parents feel that you, and perhaps your other siblings, are spending too much time on the phone, they will probably set down some rules. These could range from setting up specific times when you can make calls—such as after dinner, after having done your homework, and before your bedtime—to how much time each call should last (an hour is pushing it). Some parents might decide to let you have your own private phone line. If they are feeling really generous, they might even pay for it. Of course, if you feel your parents are being too strict and are not letting you talk at all on the phone, you can suggest having your own line. You can even offer to pay half or all of the charges. That will show them how responsible you can be.

## The Internet

Right up there with television and telephones is the Internet. As more kids have access to computers and learn how to surf the Net, more cyberaddicts are being born every day. Like television, the Internet can be a great source of both information and entertainment. It also contains a lot of violent and sexual material that is not put out there for kids your age. Like a telephone, the Internet is a great way to communicate with your friends and to find information. However, endless cyber-surfing can also tie up the phone line and distract you from other things that you need to do (remember homework?). Because of these downsides to the Net, it makes sense that your parents try to set some rules about how and when you log on.

You should also be aware that though it might be fun to meet new friends in chat rooms, you do have to be cautious in your communications, especially in terms of giving out personal information. Your parents may come up with strict rules in terms of your Internet and e-mail communications. And however unfair this may seem (after all, it is exciting to meet new people online), there have been many cases where kids your age have met up with their new supposed friends, only to find themselves in dangerous situations. So when your parents say that they don't want you to meet up with your cyberfriend unless you are accompanied by an adult, listen up. They may be saving you from trouble.

## Snacking

Coming home after school and enjoying a homemade cookie and a glass of milk is a

The Internet is a great source of information and entertainment, but spending too much time on-line can be a problem.

Most of us enjoy a snack, but eating excessive amounts of junk food can be unhealthy.

classic image of a North American childhood. Unfortunately, the image is more fiction than fact. The fact is that many kids come home from school and want to relax. And all too frequently, snacking is associated with relaxing. Often, when kids come home from school, they plop themselves in front of the television and grab a bag of chips. Then, before they know it, they have demolished the whole bag. No wonder 50 percent of American kids are overweight. In fact, American kids are the overweight champs of the world (Canadian kids are catching up to their large neighbors to the south). And this is not because of gland problems. It's because of eating poorly and eating too much.

Parents usually have rules about what their kids should and shouldn't eat. And if you look at the statistics, you can see why it is important to have such rules in place. Junk food should be limited. So should eating between

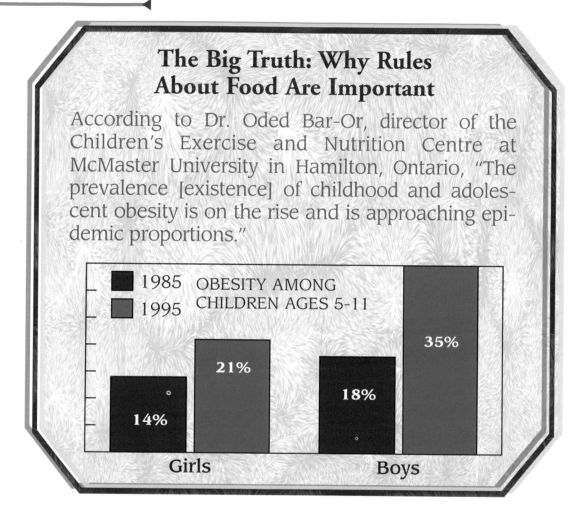

## The Big Truth: Why Rules About Food Are Important

According to Dr. Oded Bar-Or, director of the Children's Exercise and Nutrition Centre at McMaster University in Hamilton, Ontario, "The prevalence [existence] of childhood and adolescent obesity is on the rise and is approaching epidemic proportions."

OBESITY AMONG CHILDREN AGES 5-11

1985
1995

Girls: 14% (1985), 21% (1995)
Boys: 18% (1985), 35% (1995)

meals. This is because eating between meals ruins your appetite. It can become a bad habit that leads to excessive weight gain. Not to mention that it's rude if someone goes to the trouble of preparing a nice dinner, but beforehand you go to McDonald's and stock up on Big Macs.

## Household Safety

In many ways, hanging out and playing at home is safer than playing in a park or in the streets. At home you don't

As you probably know, letting a stranger into your home is not a good idea.

have to worry about cars and traffic, muggers, bullies, and attacking pit bulls. Your home is safe and familiar and there is usually someone older around whom you can run to if anything serious happens.

However, certain types of accidents can happen when you're horsing around at home. And often, your parents will set down a few rules that, even though they might seem strict, are mostly about keeping you, your family, and your home safe.

Some safety rules are common knowledge. By your age you probably know that you shouldn't play with electrical sockets, stoves, knives, or matches. You shouldn't open the door to strangers. And if your parents keep any kind of gun in the house, you should never, ever handle it without your parents' permission and supervision. Way too many kids shoot themselves, their friends, or their siblings by accident.

# 3 Away from Home

As we discussed earlier, if you live at home with one or both parents, you have to accept that they are entitled to make up rules in their house. As you get older, you will gain more independence and freedom. This means that you will begin to spend more time away from home: at extracurricular school activities, at clubs, hanging out in parks or malls or at friends' houses. On evenings and weekends, you might go out to movies, restaurants, and parties.

Of course, your parents aren't going to tag along to supervise you. And if you're at school or at a friend's house, your parents aren't the ones making the rules. Your parents will expect you to do what is right based on the rules you have learned at home. If they give you permission to do things outside the house, it is because your parents trust you and believe that you are responsible enough to make independent decisions

As you get older, you will gain more independence and spend more time away from home. It is important for you to make responsible choices and try and do what's right.

and follow other rules. Every time you break a rule—whether at home, at school, in a store, or at a friend's house—you will be convincing your parents (and others) that you are not responsible enough to be independent. Breaking rules can lead to your parents setting down new, stricter rules. It is up to you to prove that you can follow rules. This is the best way of convincing your parents to ease up on strict limits and give you more freedom.

## Safety First

Parents worry about their kids' safety. They don't want you running around day and night doing whatever you want and possibly getting into trouble. You probably don't want that either. Everybody needs boundaries. In fact, it is proven that kids whose parents set no rules or limits are unhappy. They sometimes think that their parents don't care about them. Often, kids get into trouble because they don't know how to place limits on their own behavior.

Because they want you to be safe, your parents might establish certain rules such as curfews or calling home if you think you'll be late for dinner. Your parents want you to be independent. But learning how to deal with independence takes time.

*Rennie was excited when she was invited to Lisa's party. She only hoped her mom would let her go. Ever since Rennie's stepdad had left, her mom* had been really down on boys and men. Especially when she had been drinking.

Sure enough, when Rennie asked permission, her mom asked if there would be boys there.

"Probably," murmured Rennie.

"What do you mean 'probably'?" demanded Mrs. Macintosh, taking a sip of whisky. "Yes or no?"

"Yes," said Rennie.

"You're too young to be hanging out with boys at parties. Boys are bad news. Especially at parties where drugs and drinking are involved."

"Look, Mom," said Rennie. "Lisa's dad is going to be at home. And there's not going to be any drinking or drugs. If it makes you feel better, I'll give you Mr. McCarthy's number and you can call him. And if you let me go, I promise to be home by midnight."

"Midnight! Are you crazy?" exclaimed Mrs. Macintosh. "If I let you go, you better be home by 10:00."

"How about 11:00?" tried Rennie.

"Alright, alright, alright," conceded Mrs. Macintosh. "But if you're more than ten minutes late, that's the last party you'll ever go to."

## Curfews

Many parents give their kids curfews. You might think it unfair that you have to be home from a party or dance at 10:00 PM when your best friend gets to stay out until 11:00. But different parents have different rules. If you think your parents are being unfair, talk to them. Ask them if they have specific reasons why you should be home at 10:00 and not 11:00. If they don't have specific reasons, offer an alternative curfew. Or you can try to negotiate.

>    *Marlon wanted to go and see Lenny Kravitz in concert. But the concert wouldn't be over until 11:00 PM and Marlon's curfew was 10:00.*
>    *"Aw come on, Dad," Marlon pleaded with his father.*
>    *"Mar, the last time I let you stay out until 11:30, you showed up closer to midnight."*
>    *"Yeah, I know. I lost track of time."*
>    *"You have a watch."*
>    *"Listen," said Marlon to his dad. "Why don't you give me a trial 11:30 curfew. Just for two weeks. If I'm late once, we automatically go back to 10:00. No griping. I'll even draw up a contract on the computer to make it all official."*
>    *"Yeah, okay," grumbled Marlon's dad. "I guess if it's in writing, I'll be safe."*

## Lateness

Most people are late from time to time. Some people make a bad habit of it. Out there in the real world, lateness can be a problem. Adults who are late for work too often can get fired. Students who are late for school too often can get suspended.

Obviously if you are late in getting home from a party, a friend's house, or the park, your parents aren't

Lateness can be a bad habit. Try to obey the curfews set by your parents.

going to fire you or suspend you. However, if they are sitting around the dinner table waiting for you while your dad's tuna casserole gets cold, they are not going to be pleased.

If you're expected to be home at a certain time, be there. If you're going to be late, call. Most parents will calm way down if they feel you were considerate enough to take the time to let them know that the football game went over time or that you stopped by Marcia's house to check out her new hamster.

## Nasty Habits

Smoking, drinking, and drugs are nasty habits. All can be dangerous, expensive, and highly addictive, especially if you get started at a young age when you have less experience and less resistance. Furthermore, underage drinking and use of drugs are illegal. If your parents have rules forbidding you to drink and do drugs, they are not being unfair or super strict. They are only abiding by the rules of society, which sees these activities as criminal.

In terms of smoking, parents are concerned with your health. It is scientifically proven that smoking is one of the leading causes of death in the United States. If your parents get on your case because they smell cigarette smoke on your clothes, know that they are not just trying to boss you around. Chances are they care about you living a full and healthy life.

Some parents don't want their kids going places where they feel drugs and alcohol will be around.

Sometimes their worries are valid, sometimes not. As you probably know, drugs and alcohol are all over the place—at school, in the streets—and you can't just spend your life hiding out in your basement. If your parents don't want you drinking or taking drugs, prove that you are reliable and trustworthy. Even if you go to a party where you think some kids might be drinking or smoking, don't get pressured into joining in if you know that it's going against your parents' rules. Usually, if your parents know that they can rely on you, they'll ease up on their worrying and strictness. However, if you come home sloshed one night or reeking of pot, how good will your chances be of getting permission to go out the next time?

# 4 Getting Along with Your Family

If people are going to get along with each other, they need rules. What would your classes at school be like if there were no regulations against fighting and no rule about putting up your hand before talking? Rules are equally important at home. And they go both ways. Although your parents have the right to make rules, so do you. After all, you are a part of the household, too.

## Privacy

Everybody needs some time alone in a space that is their own. This is really important in a house or apartment where many people live together in close quarters.

From time to time, your parents or siblings will want to be by themselves in their rooms. If they have rules about you not barging in without knocking, not interrupting them during a phone call, or not waking them up before 10:00 AM on a Sunday morning, then respect their rules and wishes. Similarly, stay out of your little sister's diary and out of your older brother's knapsack. Without their permission, you are invading their privacy.

Of course, privacy is a two-way street. As you start to move up in your teen years, part of your new independence will include wanting some privacy at home. To make sure that your family respects your privacy, you might want to establish some rules, too. Although you can't ban your parents and siblings from your room, you can ask them not to enter without knocking first if the door is closed. You are entitled to ask them not to go through your private things, not to read your e-mail, and not to listen in on your phone calls. Some parents have trouble accepting their kids' growing independence. Others might be snoopy or distrustful. Unless you have given them good reason to have these attitudes, they have no right to break your rules of privacy. Unfortunately, short of talking to them and even getting angry, there is not a lot you can do about snoopy parents.

It is important to respect the privacy of other family members.

## Politeness

It seems as if adults are always complaining about kids not being polite. They like to talk about how "back in my day" nobody swore and everybody said "Please, sir" and "Thank you, ma'am." Well, for better or for worse, times have changed. And so have manners and the use of language. In general, American society has become more laid-back and casual. And certain slang expressions have become the norm. Nonetheless, your parents might expect certain forms of politeness from you, both in and outside of your home. They want you to be well respected, well educated, and well liked. Knowing how to act appropriately in many different situations is part of this.

Sometimes, your parents might have very definite ideas about how they want you to behave if their friends come over, if you go visit some relatives, or if an important person calls on the telephone. You might be familiar with some of these rules: "Don't swear," "Don't pick your nose," "Don't talk with your mouth full," "Don't leave someone's house without saying 'thank you' and 'good-bye,'" "Don't fight with your little brother in public," "Keep your voice down," "Don't leave the table before everybody has finished eating," "Don't eat with your hands," "Don't stick your finger in your ear," and that's just a small sample. Parents like you to be polite because not only do your good manners make you look good, it makes them look good as parents as well.

Of course, if you're expected to act in a mature and in-control adult manner, your parents should be willing to do the same. They shouldn't yell at you in public. They shouldn't swear, pick their noses, or leave the table before everybody has finished eating either. If you're expected to speak nicely and politely to their friends on the phone or in the house, then your parents should always treat your friends with the same consideration and respect.

## Cleanliness

Aside from politeness, parents also seem to go on a great deal about cleanliness. And you have to admit that they might just have a point. Even the most well-mannered, courteous, charming ten- or twelve-year-old will have a hard time making a good impression if his hair is uncombed, his jeans have big holes, his elbows are dirty, his breath stinks, and his room looks like a pigsty. If you are not measuring up to your parents' standards in

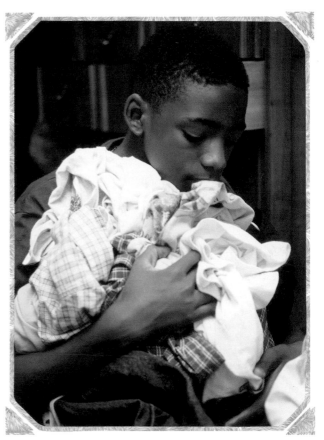

Your parents may insist that you live up to their standards of cleanliness.

If you think your parents are being too strict or uptight, try to explain your point of view and reach a compromise.

the neat-and-tidy category, they might feel obliged to set down some rules. Some of the most common include "Wash your hands before coming to the table," "Don't go out wearing dirty, wrinkly, or ripped clothes," "Change your socks and underwear every day," "Make your bed," "Clean up your room," "Hang up your clothes," "Wash out the bathtub," "Don't throw stuff on the floor," and "Rinse your dishes." Once again, these are only a few examples.

You might get tired of their nagging, but nobody wants to live in a dirty or messy house. More important, nobody wants to clean up somebody else's dirt and mess. And shutting the door to your bedroom and telling your parents to keep out if they don't want to see any tornado zones is not a useful solution.

Being clean and tidy is just as important as being polite and well mannered. This is how others judge you. And indirectly they judge your parents, too.

Of course, some parents might be inflexible or traditional. They might object to a son who wears really baggy cargo pants or a daughter who wears a very mini miniskirt. Naturally, different clothes are suitable for different occasions. But what your parents might see as sloppy, you might view as cool. If you think your parents are being uptight, try to explain your point of view. If they persist and forbid you to wear the things you like, try negotiating. Say you won't wear these clothes to school or when you go out as a family, but that you'd like to wear them on casual occasions when you go out with your friends or on weekends.

Often, compromises work because both sides feel they are giving and getting something. If you remember this rule, life will definitely be a lot easier.

# Glossary

**addiction**   Dependence on a substance such as drugs or alcohol.

**allowance**   The giving of a fixed sum of money.

**chores**   Tasks or jobs that are done around the home.

**compromise**   When two parties each give something up in order to resolve their differences.

**conflict**   Disagreement or fight.

**curfew**   Set hour to be at home at night.

**enforce**   To carry out.

**essential**   Something that is necessary.

**iguana**   Large species of lizard.

**negotiate**   To bargain with someone in order to reach an agreement.

**valid**   Something that is worthwhile or just.

# Where to Go for Help

## In the United States

Big Brothers Big Sisters of America
230 North 13th Street
Philadelphia, PA 19107
(215) 567-7000
e-mail: national@bbbsa.org
Web site: http://www.bbbsa.org

Families Anonymous
P.O. Box 3457
Culver City, CA 90231-3457
(800) 736-9805
(310) 313-5800
e-mail: famanon@aol.com

# In Canada

Big Brothers and Sisters of Canada
3228 South Service Road, Suite 112E
Burlington, ON L7N 3H8
(800) 263-9133
(905) 639-0461
e-mail: BBSCMaster@aol.com
Web site: http://www.bbsc.ca

# Web Sites

About Teens Now
http://www.aboutteensnow.com

Living with Parents
http://www.fcs.wa.gov.au/parenting/lwp

UCB Parents Advice about Teenagers
http://parents.berkeley.edu/advice/teens

# For Further Reading

Corwin, Donna G. *The Tween Years.* Lincolnwood, IL: Contemporary Books, 1998.

Keltner, Nancy, ed. *If You Print This, Please Don't Use My Name: Questions from Teens and Their Parents About Things that Matter.* Norwich, VT: Terra Nova Press, 1992.

Kimball, Gayle. *The Teen Trip: The Complete Resource Guide.* Chico, CA: Equality Press, 1996.

Mosatche, Harriet S., and Karen Unger. *Too Old for This, Too Young for That.* Minneapolis: Free Spirit Publishing, 2000.

Packer, Alex J. *Bringing Up Parents: The Teenager's Handbook.* Minneapolis: Free Spirit Publishing, 1992.

Pollack, William S., and Todd Shuster. *Real Boys' Voices.* New York: Random House, 2000.

# Index

## ABOUT THE AUTHOR

Lea MacAdam grew up in Topeka, Kansas before moving to New York City. She works as a freelance writer and photographer and is single-handedly raising two (mostly) rule-abiding children.

## PHOTO CREDITS

Cover and interior shots by Ira Fox.

## DESIGN

Geri Giordano